The North Ocean

Nick Monks

Credits- Front cover photo of Fairhaven, Lytham St Annes-
By the author

Doc Leaf Imprint

For Amanda, Karl, Saskia

Title Page

Published August 2022

The North Ocean -Nick Monks

Bluebell Publishing/ Doc Leaf Imprint

Printed by Lulu
www.lulu.com

ISBN- 978-1-4710-7205-5

CONTENTS

1

Fiona, Scottish Borders   Page 7

Evening   8

Night   9

Flood   10

Leaving to Return   11

11

Blackhouse   19

The Sea, The Sea   21

Walkers, Morecambe   22

She   23

Antarctic Ocean   26

The Pacific   28

The North Ocean

Fiona, Scottish Borders

Within the renovated stone croft

She stoops and kneads bread dough

Her hands pound the bread mix

Shadows form across the floor and walls

She is a princess of the mountains

The north ocean swells and covers the granite

The waves roar in and segment

We are on the shore with limpets and sea urchins

The house burgeons with beads and shells and Celtic

Nimbus crosses

As the bread is shaped and placed in the oven

The sky is a patchwork of light and sepia blue clouds

She turns. Slight, with blond hair and sapphire eyes.

Evening

At evening when the work is done

She tarries by the lounge fire

Her hair is done up in tattered whisps

She wears a large buckle on her belt

She carries the day as water and clay

She erases nothingness. And bequeaths

Forests of finches and squirrels

And an infinity of mountain peaks.

Night

At night. The river by the front door

Carries us away to the valley lake

She sleeps in a Lithuanian forest

I sleep in a blue teeming city

James Hogg's ghost startles me on the landing

The hens roust in the fox free tree branches

And the shadows and stillness erase New York

And on a bed of bracken I visit Anwynn.

Flood

Thousands of damsel flies flood the stream

The day is clear and dressed in Oxfam rags

I drive to Galashiels

And the north ocean burgeons and tears at the rocks

Bramblings and siskin feed at the bird table

As I dig four shallow trenches for a greenhouse

And she calls from the ruined castle.

Leaving to Return

When I left. To return to my books

The roads were foretold

And the homecoming to Dove cottage

Was between two homes. We had travelled

Back to William Blakes London. And Keats wanderings

I spent the next two years always seeking the shore

And gazing in bafflement at the sea/ sky horizon.

Credit- Pexels- Andrew Neel- 7174579

Credit- Pexels – Mitchell Henderson- 2004388

11

Blackhouse

(Scottish Borders, former residence of poet James Hogg 1770 to 1835. "The Ettrick Shepherd")

The snow slips down on Christmas day

We have been marooned by snow for one month

Her face on the mountain slopes in summer and winter

The sky knows no one's names. A gossamer duvet

Love starts again, the finches in the woods

The fire warms us, guitars resound in the mountains

A snipe zig zags to paradise. Then the snow and snow

A nought nestled cottage, becomes a one

You see here in the Border mountains, there are no cities

Between here and the North Ocean

Snow buttercup, sun, Brambling wings

To bleach the north with orange

Then love begins again, with dawn and snow

Rice like bread like wine like incense like grass

A gale of clouds and waiting, and icicles of hope

Looking into her face on the mountain slopes.

The Sea, The Sea

Ocean yearns and heaves

the stars burn holes in the water

dark, ceaseless, it is the music

of harmony, salt pollen tearing

at the horizon.

Walkers, Morecambe

Sunday, a woman struggles with an umbrella

Coat collar turned to the cold, dressed in green and black

Her kids, two of them follow in indiscipline

My emptiness longing to be part of the photo

But they are gone, the jetty and me

Wishing towards the silver slither of sea

Silhouetted on the beach an elderly couple in unison

Bent under the sheet of sky, in rays of light

Attachments for now are as far away

As a birds call over the arctic

Meandering I observe, kelp, cockles, razor shells

Walk on the lace of sand, walking to not go anywhere.

She

Her black soft hair

cannot be contained

in this poem

to the cry of the gull

the shell in the sand

where

Within an islands contours

lies the love

beyond loves

I do not desire her

how can the air

be desired

But the air we both

breathe is between us, cannot

be escaped

Like singularity

her black

hair burning

on a peninsular

of towards

stretching

of towards where

who, perhaps just

towards

I hold a ticket

and throw it to the

ocean wind

In a dream of

a mind, that resounds

to no music

Save the music

of a future contained within

the past

Like the world

in the vortex of

a shell

In a cove of

distant dreams

delicate.

Antarctic Ocean

Your swimming breaststroke

Like in the municipal pool

The water is so cold it hurts

You cannot see beyond- you are submerged in the water

You stumble to appraise

Nervously drink the sea in your lungs

Your last moments of life

The sky a cold amphitheatre of belonging

The laughter of leopard seals, penguins and orcas

The judicial mercy of Antarctic blue- eyed snow mermaids

Green red teethed sea serpents, blue effervescent ghost fish

Skuas and petrels and terns wing beats

With terrifying black berry eyes

All more adept here than James Dyer swimming alone

The water is like a freezing venomous enamored cloak

It is so beautiful and peaceful

So deliciously and desired alone

You're the only person for 1000's of miles

A white albatross flaps by uninterested

You would like to be above;

To savor the hurt of the steel grey bathosphere

To map the divine beauty of the grey Antarctica

You resentful there's no southern wave tempest/ storm

Swim forward in the hope of solid ice ahead

Then by mistake you breathe in water

In a millisecond after an instant of precious hope

Your last glimpse of the disappearing albatross

You frantically gulp more water to try and clear your throat

Before the plunge of the Antarctic oceans

Beautiful, stunning, steel grey grave, tinged with purple/

Greenness.

The Pacific

So much turmoil, blazing waves

Into the ether of air, salt pain

Waves spent on the shore, another

Then another, eternity

Fractured waters, aquiline

That rejoin again under

The blank indifference of the moon

The talcum powder of the sand

I taste the bitter sharp salt

Catch waves like sails

In the fabric of the dark sky

That falls to the sea, the horizons.

Morecambe Bay from north shore

Fairhaven, Lytham coast

Fairhaven, Lytham, Lancashire

Nick Monks lives near Preston, Lancashire, UK. He studied philosophy at Hull University. Has worked in scores of careers. Spent about seven years traveling the world.

His poems have appeared in numerous UK magazines and a few international. He has self-published about 144 pamphlets and books.

Milton Keynes UK
Ingram Content Group UK Ltd.
UKHW050211301223
435210UK00002B/5